ENERGY EFFICIENT ROUTING MODEL FOR REMOTE SYSTEMS IN WIRELESS NETWORKS

ENERGY EFFICIENT ROUTING MODEL FOR REMOTE SYSTEMS IN WIRELESS NETWORKS

SINDHUJA M.

ELIVA PRESS

ISBN: 978-99949-8-985-0

Cover Design: Eliva Press
Cover Image: Ingimage
Email: info@elivapress.com
Website: www.elivapress.com

This Eliva Press imprint is published by the registered company Eliva Press Global Ltd. part of Eliva Press S.R.L. Publishing Group

The registered company address is: Pope Hennessy Street Level 2, Hennessy Tower Port Louis, Mauritius
Eliva Press S.R.L. Publishing Group address is: Bulevardul Moscova 21, Chisinau, Moldova, Europe

CHAPTER 1

RESOURCE AWARE SYSTEM

1.1. Abstract

The sensors in the WSN gather information and convey it to a destination hub. A large portion of the current recommendations manage the activity stream issue to convey information to the destination hub in a vitality effective way. In the manuscript, the issue has been amplified into a multi-destination case. Both of the issues are figured by the linear programming model to ideal areas of the multiple destination hubs and the ideal activity stream rate of directing ways in remote sensor systems. The enhanced lifetime and reasonableness of the plan are contrasted and those of the multi-destination aware least profundity tree conspire. A practical power utilization model of remote correspondence subsystems ordinarily utilized as a part of numerous sensors arrange hub gadgets is introduced. Basic power utilization models for significant segments are separately distinguished, and the compelling transmission scope of a sensor hub is demonstrated by the yield force of the transmitting power intensifier, affectability of the accepting low commotion enhancer and other condition. Utilizing the fundamental model, conditions for least sensor arrange control utilization are inferred for correspondence of sensor information from a source gadget to a goal hub. Control utilization demonstrates parameters are extricated for two sorts of remote sensor hubs that are generally utilized and monetarily accessible. Promote thought of correspondence convention overhead likewise demonstrates that solitary jump steering will be more power effective contrasted with multi-bounce directing under sensible conditions. The power utilization model can be utilized to guide outline decisions at a wide range of layers of the plan space including, topology plan, hub situation, vitality effective directing plans, control administration and the equipment plan of future WSN entities. Definition with Occurrence to Destination Stable Transport (ODST) Protocol in Wireless Sensor Networks has been talked about.

Keywords: Wireless Sensor Network, Congestion, Integer Linear Programming, Occurrence to Destination Stable Transport (ODST) Protocol, Multi-destination aware Minimum Depth Tree, Energy, Power.

1.2. Introduction

In a Wireless Sensor Networks, every sensor hub has a little detecting scope and a little correspondence run-in light of the fact that expanding the detecting scope and correspondence range would expend more battery power. Since every sensor hub has a little correspondence go, every sensor hub transfers the detected occasions to a destination hub. As the quantity of destination hubs is expanded, the way length from sensor hub to destination hub is diminished and the lifetime of the sensor hubs is expanded [2]. Be that as it may, the quantity of destination hub is obliged fiscally on the grounds that the cost of the destination hub is costlier than the sensor hub. There has been much research done on activity designing in wired systems. The principal motivation behind movement building is to expand the connection usage by similarly adjusting the activity over the system. It is additionally conceivable to apply the activity designing in a remote sensor arrange. Be that as it may, the reason ought to be to expand the system lifetime as opposed to enhancing the connection usage, in light of the fact that the basic asset of remote sensor systems is the battery force of the sensor hub rather than the connection data transfer capacity despite the fact that the destination hubs don't have a vitality imperative since they are associated with a wired system [5]. Previously, most investigates concentrated on the vitality protection. As of late, a few reviews handle finding the multiple destinations in extensive scale remote sensor arranges and enhancing the situation of incorporation focuses in multi-bounce remote systems, however any of manuscripts did not consider activity designing. In the manuscript, a plan is proposed to enhance the lifetime and the reasonableness of remote sensor connects with multiple destination hubs. It has been accepted that the remote sensor organize demonstrates the bunch design. In the engineering, the group header has information sending usefulness. The proposed details take care of two issues, the area of destination hubs and the movement stream rates of directing ways in the remote sensor organize.

It has been figured that the present issue into two sorts of straight projects. In the principal detailing, it is accepted that the area and the quantity of the destination hubs are settled. The arrangement of the primary direct projects definition demonstrates the ideal movement stream rates of steering ways in the remote sensor organize. In the second straight projects plan, rather than expecting the pre-settled area and number of the destination hubs, the requirement of the greatest number of destination hubs is just accepted [7]. For the situation, the arrangement of the direct projects plan finds both the ideal area of destination hubs and the ideal movement stream rates of steering ways in remote sensor organize. The primary concentration is the second straight projects definition. It is demonstrated that the proposed definition expands the lifetime and the reasonableness of a remote sensor organize by utilizing program that is a kind of Integer Linear Programming solver.

CHAPTER 2

RELATED WORKS

In the past research, the Pump Slowly, Fetch Quickly component is proposed for solid reinventing in Wireless Sensor Networks. Pump Slowly, Fetch Quickly depends on gradually infusing parcels into the system, yet performing forceful jump by-bounce recuperation if there should be an occurrence of bundle misfortunes. The pump operation in Pump Slowly, Fetch Quickly essentially performs controlled flooding and requires each transitional hub to make and keep up an information reserve to be utilized for nearby misfortune recuperation and in-arrangement information conveyance. In spite of the fact that this is an imperative transport layer answer for Wireless Sensor Networks, it is pertinent just for strict sensor-to-sensor dependability and for motivations behind control and administration in the switch heading from the destination to sensor hubs. Henceforth, the utilization of Pump Slowly, Fetch Quickly for the forward bearing can prompt a misuse of important assets. Likewise, Pump Slowly, Fetch Quickly does not deliver parcel misfortunes because of blockage [8]. In the prior research, the Reliable Multi-Segment Transport convention is proposed to address the necessities of dependable information transport in Wireless Sensor Networks. Reliable Multi-Segment Transport is chiefly in light of the functionalities given by coordinated dissemination. Moreover, Reliable Multi-Segment Transport uses in-system storing and gives ensured conveyance of the information bundles created by the occasion streams. Nonetheless, occasion discovery and additionally following does not require ensured end-to-end information conveyance since the individual information streams are corresponded misfortune tolerant.

In addition, such ensured unwavering quality by means of in-system reserving may bring critical overhead for the sensor systems with power and preparing confinements. Interestingly, Occurrence to Destination Stable Transport Protocol (ODST) depends on an occasion to-destination unwavering quality model and gives solid occasion discovery with no transitional reserving prerequisites. Occurrence to Destination Stable Transport Protocol (ODST) additionally tries to accomplish the required occasion recognition precision utilizing least vitality consumption and has a blockage control part [9]. Then again, transport arrangements in different remote systems mostly concentrate on solid information transport taking after end-to-end Transport Control Protocol semantics and are proposed to address the difficulties postured by remote connection mistakes and portability. The essential purpose behind their inapplicability in Wireless Sensor Networks is their thought of end-to-end dependability. Besides, every one of these conventions conveys significant memory necessities to support transmitted parcels until they are recognized by the recipient. Interestingly, sensor hubs have constrained buffering space and handling abilities. Thus, there is a requirement for a novel transport instrument in Wireless Sensor

Networks that underscores on Collective dependability, asset productivity and straightforwardness.

Regardless of the significant measure of research on a few parts of sensor systems administration, the issues of solid transport and clog control are yet to be effectively examined and tended to. The earnest requirement for blockage control is called attention to inside the dialog of foundation exchange offs for Wireless Sensor Networks. Be that as it may, the creators don't propose any answer for the issue they distinguish [12]. In another current work, the Pump Slowly, Fetch Quickly system is proposed for solid reinventing in Wireless Sensor Networks. Pump Slowly, Fetch Quickly depends on gradually infusing bundles into the system, however performing forceful jump by-bounce recuperation if there should arise an occurrence of parcel misfortune. The pump operation in Pump Slowly, Fetch Quickly just performs controlled requires each middle of the road hub to make and keep up an information reserve to be utilized for neighbourhood misfortune recuperation and in-grouping information conveyance. Despite the fact that this is a vital transport layer answer for Wireless Sensor Networks, it is appropriate just for strict sensor-to-sensor unwavering quality and for motivations behind control and administration in the turnaround course from the destination to sensor hubs. Occasion recognition and additionally following in the forward heading does not require ensured end-to-end information conveyance as in Pump Slowly, Fetch Quickly. Singular information owes are related and misfortune tolerant to the degree that coveted occasion components are on the whole and dependably educated to the destination [14]. Thus, the utilization of Pump Slowly, Fetch Quickly for the forward course can prompt a misuse of profitable assets. Moreover, Pump Slowly, Fetch Quickly does not deliver parcel misfortune because of clog. Conversely, Occurrence to Destination Stable Transport Protocol (ODST) depends on an occasion to-destination unwavering quality model and gives solid occasion location with no transitional storing necessities. Occurrence to Destination Stable Transport Protocol (ODST) additionally looks to accomplish the required occasion location exactness utilizing least vitality use and has a blockage control part [1]. A novel transmission control conspires for use at the Medium Access Controller layer in Wireless Sensor Networks is proposed with the primary target of per hub reasonable data transfer capacity share. Vitality proficiency is kept up by controlling the rate at which MAC layer infuses parcels into the channel. Albeit such an approach can control the transmission rate of a sensor hub, it neither considers clog control nor addresses dependable occasion location. Next, the transport arrangements are considered in different remote systems and bring up their insufficiencies when connected to Wireless Sensor Networks. These reviews fundamentally concentrate on dependable information transport taking after end-to-end TCP semantics and are proposed to address the difficulties postured by remote connection blunders and portability.

The multi-jump and many-to-one nature of information streams in Wireless Sensor Networks prompts an audit of dependable multicast arrangements proposed in other wired/remote systems. There exist numerous such plans that address the dependable transport and clog control for the instance of single sender and multiple recipients [3]. In spite of the fact that the correspondence structure of the turnaround way, i.e., from destination to sources in Wireless Sensor Networks, is a case of multicast, it is not substantial for the forward channel where multiple related reports are sent to a solitary goal. Comparative transport issues with multiple senders and a solitary beneficiary in other wired/remote systems just relates to a multiple unicast. Nonetheless, the Wireless Sensor Networks worldview requires the thought of aggregate unwavering quality. Subsequently, neither the dependable multicast nor unicast transport arrangements can be connected for the situation.

CHAPTER 3

OVERVIEW OF EXISTING SYSTEM

Broad arrangements of Wireless Sensor Networks in brilliant urban areas and their interoperability with cell phones empower a few intriguing collaborations. The principal inspiration is to bolster a financially savvy acknowledgment of wide-scale urban checking applications. The run of the mill instance of auxiliary checking applications exhibited as reference situation is portrayed by necessities and components that are regular to any observing application where alert circumstances show separated desperation levels; the proposition suits those conditions.

Since correspondence amongst wireless ad hoc network (WANET) and Wireless Sensor Networks could empty valuable vitality assets out of Wireless Sensor Networks hubs, a significant indicate is plan arrangements and conventions that limit wireless ad hoc network (WANET)-Wireless Sensor Networks associations, by empowering them just for critical information conveyance. While it has effectively tended to a portion of the issues of the Wireless Sensor Networks-wireless ad hoc network (WANET) coordination from the Wireless Sensor Networks point of view in the past work, the article concentrates on the wireless ad hoc network (WANET) side. Thus, in whatever is left of the manuscript all fundamental coordination are gathered in detailed and grouping capacities acknowledged at wireless ad hoc network (WANET) hubs for Wireless Sensor Networks-wireless ad hoc network (WANET) joining in IoT arrangement conditions [4]. The segment has been concluded by drawing the conceptual reference display and by giving some required foundation material. The dispersed design incorporates two fundamental system layers: at the lower level, Wireless Sensor Networks sensor hubs frame an independent steering layer that conveys ordinary/dire information to at least one roots; at the more elevated amount, multi-homed portable wireless ad hoc network (WANET) hubs wander over the Wireless Sensor Networks-prepared condition. A tree-based information gathering for Wireless Sensor Networks has been expected: tree-like topologies for Wireless Sensor Networks information directing have been broadly utilized in both exploratory conventions [6]. Along these lines, a non-specific tree-based convention is chosen in the work to effortlessly empower its organization and quick use with all rising gathering arrangements and standard determinations, conceivably one-sided toward innovations that uniquely in contrast to IEEE 802.15.4, don't experience the ill effects of obstructions with existing together IEEE 802.11 systems utilized by wireless ad hoc network (WANET) hubs. The tree development and information steering function as takes after.

For the most part, information roots begin promoting a zero cost, while each inner hub publicizes an aggregate incremental cost, equivalent to the cost of its dad hub in addition to the cost of the connection to the following jump; information parcels stream along ways toward lower cost hubs [10]. The Wireless Sensor

Networks level craftily misuses its wireless ad hoc network (WANET) hubs in perceivability to make the extra low-inertness high-transfer speed overlay for dire information directing. To stick together Wireless Sensor Networks and wireless ad hoc network (WANET)s, wireless ad hoc network (WANET) hubs misuse their Wireless Sensor Networks interfaces to partake to earnest information directing by progressively finding Wireless Sensor Networks hubs amid their meandering and by promoting their nearness to them. To defeat versatility and adaptability issues run of the mill of huge and thick wireless ad hoc network (WANET)wireless ad hoc network (WANET) arrangements, the requirement are guaranteed for novel arrangements and models to sort out wireless ad hoc network (WANET) hubs in little nearby bunches. For simple coherence and introduction clearness, let us characterize here some valuable terms. Roots are sensor hubs that promote themselves as gathering tree roots, commonly going about as passages to the Internet. All other sensor hubs manufacture directing trees to forward gathered information toward roots at the Wireless Sensor Networks layer [11]. A Wireless Sensor Networks leave point is any Wireless Sensor Networks hub in perceivability of no less than one wireless ad hoc network (WANET) hub and ready to hop earnest information over the wireless ad hoc network (WANET), while a Wireless Sensor Networks section point is the Wireless Sensor Networks hub with the least slope cost that the wireless ad hoc network (WANET) bunch can reach. At long last, wireless ad hoc network (WANET) passage and ways out focuses are wireless ad hoc network (WANET) hubs that can individually get/forward information from/to the Wireless Sensor Networks [13]. The answer is sufficiently general to work with most tree-based sensor information accumulation principles and related research-arranged conventions. IETF RPL is an exceptionally encouraging standard particular in the field, yet at the present stage there are as yet a not very many cases of its arrangement and it experiences restricted testing in reasonable in-the-field situations.

CHAPTER 4

PROPOSED METHOD - OCCURRENCE TO DESTINATION STABLE TRANSPORT PROTOCOL (ODST)

Occurrence to Destination Stable Transport Protocol (ODST) is a novel arrangement that is proposed to address the vehicle issue in Wireless Sensor Networks. The essential thought process of Occurrence to Destination Stable Transport Protocol (ODST) is to accomplish and keep up operation in state. Thus, the point is to arrange the announcing recurrence to accomplish the coveted occasion identification exactness with least vitality use. To help fulfil this, Occurrence to Destination Stable Transport Protocol (ODST) utilizes a clog control system that fills the double need of solid discovery and vitality preservation. Thus, a productive transport convention ought to monitor the unwavering quality saw at the destination and as needs be arrange the working point. In the event that the standardized occurrence stability is inside the coveted unwavering quality points of confinement and no clog warning caution is gotten, then state has been come to and the destination illuminates source hubs to keep up the present detailing recurrence "fr" . Here, the sensible suspicion has been made that the destination is sufficiently intense to achieve all source hubs by communicate.

All in all, the system can dwell in any of the five states (s) that incorporates the accompanying:

- No Congestion, Low Dependability (NC, LD)
- No Congestion, High Dependability (NC, HD)
- High Congestion, Low Dependability (NC, LD)
- High Congestion, High Dependability (NC, HD)

Hence it can be said that the state is the sum of all as shown in equation 1.

$$S = \sum (NC, LD) | (NC, HD) | (NC, LD) | (NC, HD) \quad (1)$$

Contingent upon the present state 'Sc', Occurrence to Destination Stable Transport Protocol (ODST) computes a refreshed detailing recurrence, which is then communicate to the source hubs. For example, if state (S) incorporates No Congestion, Low Dependability (NC, LD) and High Congestion, Low Dependability (NC, LD), the watched unwavering quality levels are insufficient to distinguish the coveted occasion highlights. In such a case, Occurrence to Destination Stable Transport Protocol (ODST) forcefully refreshes the revealing recurrence to dependably track the occasion as quickly as time permits. The self-designing nature of Occurrence to Destination Stable Transport Protocol (ODST) helps it adjust to element topology and irregular organization, both run of the mill of Wireless Sensor Networks. Another vital element of Occurrence to Destination Stable Transport Protocol (ODST) is its slant to monitor rare vitality assets when dependability levels surpass those required for occasion location. The is the situation when state (S) incorporates No Congestion, Low Dependability (NC, LD) and High Congestion,

Low Dependability (NC, LD). The inspiration to decrease the announcing recurrence for the situation originates from vitality preservation. Be that as it may, the essential rationale of solid occasion identification must not be bargained. Consequently, Occurrence to Destination Stable Transport Protocol (ODST) adopts a moderate strategy for the situation and reductions f in a controlled way.

The calculations of Occurrence to Destination Stable Transport Protocol (ODST) for the most part keep running on the destination, with negligible usefulness at the source hubs. All the more correctly, sensor hubs just need the accompanying two extra functionalities Sensor hubs must tune in to the destination communicate toward the finish of every choice interim and refresh their detailing rates. Sensor hubs must convey a basic and sans overhead nearby clog discovery bolster component. While the previous is an execution issue and is not inside the extent of the work, the subtle elements of a clog discovery instrument are given. Such an elegant exchange of unpredictability from sensor hubs to the destination hub diminishes administration expenses and saves money on profitable sensor assets. Additionally streamlining execution is the way that Occurrence to Destination Stable Transport Protocol (ODST) takes a shot at the aggregate ID guideline and does not require interesting source personality.

Algorithm of the Occurrence to Destination Stable Transport Protocol (ODST) protocol operation is given below:

```
If m=1;
ODST();
If (Congestion)
If (Stability (α)<1)
Freq=Freq^(α/m);
M=m+1;
Else if (α>1)
m=1;
Freq= Freq/α;
End;
Else if (No Congestion)
m=1;
If (α<1-E(s))
Freq= Freq/α;
Else if (α>1 + E(s))
Freq=Freq/2 (1+1/ α)
Else if (1- E(s)≤ α ≤1+ E(s))
 Freq=Freq;
 End;
End;
```

Figure 1. Algorithm of the Occurrence to Destination Stable Transport Protocol (ODST) protocol operation.

Figure 1 show the algorithm of the Occurrence to Destination Stable Transport Protocol (ODST) protocol operation. Where 'm' is the number of successive decision intervals for which the network has remained in one state, 'α' is the stability of the occurrence, 'Freq' is the frequency, 'E(s)' is the element of state.

Blockage Detection has been talked about in the area. To decide the present system state "S" in Occurrence to Destination Stable Transport Protocol (ODST), the destination must have the capacity to recognize blockage in the system. However, the routine affirmation-based identification techniques for end-to-end blockage control purposes can't be connected here. The reason at the end of the day lies in the idea of occasion to-destination dependability as opposed to end-to-end unwavering quality. Just the destination, and no of the sensor hubs, can decide the stability of occurrence (α) and act as needs be. In addition, end-to-end retransmissions and affirmation over heads are a misuse of constrained sensor assets. Henceforth, Occurrence to Destination Stable Transport Protocol (ODST) utilizes a blockage identification system in light of nearby cradle level checking in sensor hubs. Any sensor hub whose steering support floods because of extreme approaching bundles is said to be congested and it educates the destination of the same.

The points of interest of the instrument are as per the following. In the occasion to-destination demonstrate, the activity produced amid each detailing period. The detailing recurrence f does not change inside one announcing period since it is controlled intermittently by the destination toward the finish of every choice interim with time of τ that is more noteworthy than the recurrence. Accordingly, the measure of approaching movement to any sensor hub in successive announcing interims is expected to remain steady. This, thusly, means the augmentation in the cradle totality level toward the finish of each announcing interim is required to be consistent. Figure 2 demonstrates a delineation of cradle level observing in sensor hubs. For a given sensor hub, let Δb be the cradle length increase saw toward the finish of last announcing period.

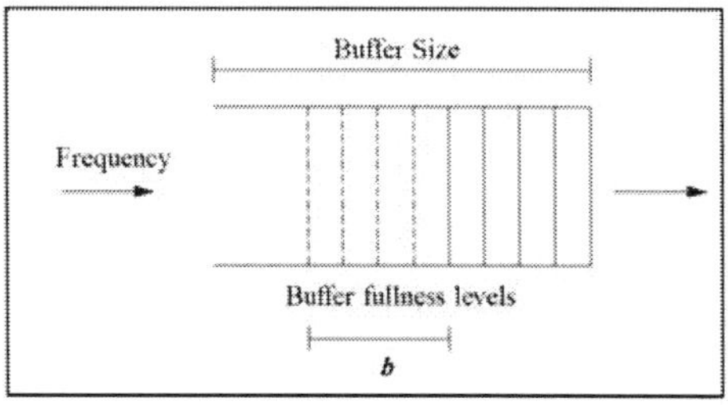

Figure 2. An illustration of buffer level monitoring in sensor nodes

Execution of Occurrence to Destination Stable Transport Protocol (ODST) is talked about here. In the area, both expository and re-enactment has been displayed comes about on the execution of Occurrence to Destination Stable Transport Protocol (ODST) convention. Occurrence to Destination Stable Transport Protocol (ODST) is self-designing in this sense and can henceforth perform proficiently under irregular, dynamic topology much of the time experienced in Wireless Sensor Networks applications. They can subsequently be deciphered as achievable lower limits. Some scientific outcomes are presented on Occurrence to Destination Stable Transport Protocol (ODST) performance relying upon the underlying system state 'Si'.

Hypothesis 1: Starting from 'Si'=No Congestion, Low Dependability (NC, LD), and with occurrence stability (α) conduct when the system is not congested, the system state stays unaltered until Occurrence to Destination Stable Transport Protocol (ODST) meets to state.

Evidence: The direct unwavering quality (α) conduct for Freq < Max.

Occurrence to Destination Stable Transport Protocol (ODST) conservatively decrements the Freq which is meant in condition 2.

$$Freq(i+1) = \frac{Freq}{2}\left(1 + \frac{1}{\alpha}\right) \qquad (2)$$

$$\alpha(i+1) = \left(\frac{1+\alpha}{2}\right) \qquad (3)$$

CHAPTER 5

FORMULATION WITH THE PROPOSED OCCURRENCE TO DESTINATION STABLE TRANSPORT PROTOCOL (ODST) ALGORITHM

The proposed plan in the manuscript considers arrange lifetime and decency. That is, under an obliged sensor hub vitality, to start with, to augment the base among information volume created by every sensor hub for guaranteeing reasonableness, and afterward to amplify add up to information volume delivered by hubs for expanding the system lifetime. The Max/Min plan is known to give great decency. The given particular system lifetime can be fulfilled by constraining sending information volume per unit time concerning introductory vitality of sensor hub. In remote framework, the power utilization of interface out of gear mode is lower than both the transmission control and the gathering power. What's more, the remote sensor hubs utilize the power sparing instrument by exchanging between dynamic state and rest state. The information transmission and in addition gathering is performed just in dynamic period and the proportion expected of dynamic period is adequately little. In the event that the area of destination hubs is settled, directing ways of every sensor hub and the information volume through every way can be acquired by Preparation 1.

Preparation for the Proposed Occurrence to Destination Stable Transport Protocol (ODST) Algorithm

$$Y_{M.N} - Y_{N.M} = Dv(M); (M \in i) \qquad (4)$$

Equation 4 defines which is data volume produced by node (M).

$$Dv(M) > 0; (M \in i) \qquad (5)$$

$$Y_{M.N} = 0; (M \in S) \qquad (6)$$

A sensor node should transmit data more than 0 bit. A destination node should not transmit any data to other sensor nodes. There should be the minimum among data volume produced by each sensor node. The total data volume produced by sensor nodes is shown in equation 7 and 8.

$$V_{Min} \leq Dv; (M \in i) \qquad (7)$$

$$V_{Tot} \leq Dv; (M, N \in i) \qquad (8)$$

$$P^{T}_{M.N} * (Y^{m}_{M.N} + P^{R})(Y^{m}_{N.M} + I_{energy}) + C; (M \in i) \qquad (9)$$

Where, Dv(M) is the Data volume of node M produces. V_{Min} is the minimum of the Data volume. V_{Tot} is the sum of the Data volume. 'i' is the sensor nodes. 's' is the destination nodes. $P^{T}_{M.N}$ is the Transmission power from node 'm' to node 'n' per unit data volume (bit). P^R is denoted as Receive power per unit data volume (bit). I_{energy} is the initial energy of a sensor node. The Formulation1 is a Linear Programming problem because the location of destination nodes is fixed, so it can be solved in polynomial time by using Linear Programming solver. Formulation1 ensures the system execution of two sorts. At the point when the V_{Min} is amplified, all sensor hubs are ensured to create the information volume of at any rate V_{Min} and to speak with destination hubs. Therefore, every sensor hub can deliver the information volume of V_{Min} paying little mind to the information volume created by other sensor hubs. At the point when the sit out of gear force of sensor hub is insignificant, the lifetime of sensor system is subject to the information volume of transmission and gathering. Subsequently, if the V_{Tot} is amplified, the lifetime of sensor system is additionally augmented. Here, the system lifetime implies the length that the batteries of all sensor hubs have been drained.

The integration of WSN and the IOT can be ordered in two diverse ways: stack-based and topology-based. In the stack-based arrangement, the level of incorporation between the Internet and a WSN relies on upon the likenesses between their system stacks. A WSN can be totally free from the Internet, have the capacity to trade data with Internet has, or share a perfect system layer convention. Then again, in the topology based grouping the level of combination relies on upon the real area of the hubs that gives access to the Internet. These hubs can be a couple of double sensor hubs situated on the base of the WSN, or an undeniable spine of gadgets that enable detecting hubs to get to the Internet in one bounce. For lucidity, the distinctive methodologies will be clarified in the accompanying sections. In the stack-based order, the principal approach is the Front-End arrangement. In this arrangement, the outer Internet has and the sensor hubs never discuss specifically with each other. Actually, the WSN is totally free from the Internet, so it can actualize its own particular arrangement of conventions. All collaborations between the outside world and the sensor system will be overseen by a unified gadget, for example, a base station. This base station can store every one of the information streams originating from the WSN, and it can likewise give these information streams to outer elements through surely understood interfaces. Moreover, any inquiries originating from Internet hosts will dependably navigate the base station. The second approach, the Gateway arrangement, considers the presence of a gadget that goes about as an application layer door, accountable for deciphering the lower layer conventions from both systems and steering the data starting with one point then onto the next. Therefore, Internet hosts and sensor hubs can have the capacity to address each other and trade data without setting up a really coordinate association.

In this arrangement, the WSN is as yet free from the Internet, and all questions still need to cross a door gadget. Be that as it may, sensor hubs can have the capacity to give web benefit interfaces to outer substances while keeping up their lower layer conventions. With respect to the third approach, the TCP/IP arrangement, sensor hubs execute the TCP/IP stack, subsequently they can be considered as undeniable components of the Internet. Any Internet host can open an immediate association with them, and vice versa. Actually, this arrangement completely coordinates the WSN with the IoT. A result of this approach is that sensor hubs are no longer ready to utilize particular WSN conventions. As to topology-based order, the Hybrid arrangement approach considers that there is an arrangement of hubs inside the WSN, normally situated at the edge of the system that can get to the Internet specifically. Actually, these hubs can be effortlessly mapped to base stations, since each sensor inside the WSN needs to navigate them keeping in mind the end goal to associate the focal framework, and vice versa. The particular components of this kind of approach are repetition and system insight. As a matter of course, this approach considers that it is conceivable to give more than one base station to get to the usefulness of the system. Furthermore, as those base stations have the ability to interface with the Internet; it implies that the insight of the system is pushed onto a subset of the WSN.

This appointment of abilities is additionally created in the Access Point arrangement approach. Here, WSNs end up noticeably lopsided trees with different roots, where leaves are typical sensor hubs and every other component of the tree are Internet-empowered hubs. Subsequently, all sensor hubs can have the capacity to get to the Internet in only one bounce. One of the primary components of this approach is the likelihood to build the abilities of hubs that have a place with the spine organize. For instance, spine hubs can have a bigger number of assets than ordinary hubs, and can execute speedier system measures. Note that the beforehand demonstrated topology-based systems are normally joined with the methodologies from the stack-based order. For instance, in a spine sort arrange, the Internet-empowered hubs can act as a front-end, adequately disengaging the WSN sensors from the Internet, or as passages, permitting direct information trade amongst sensors and the focal framework. There is a special case, however: it is basically unessential to join the TCP/IP arrangement with the cross breed and spine arrangements, as each hub will have the capacity to interface the Internet. Actually, the main errand of the hubs that interface the Internet with the neighbourhood system will be to carry on as interpreters.

CHAPTER 6

PERFORMANCE EVALUATION-RESULTS AND DISCUSSIONS

A specimen system that is utilized for re-enactment has been appeared in Figure 3 hubs are conveyed haphazardly in the framework. For the correlation with the propose plan, multi-destination aware Minimum Depth Tree is utilized. The connection cost is vitality that is devoured when unit information is transmitted through the connection. It has been realized that multi-destination aware Minimum Depth Tree can course parcels with negligible vitality utilization. The recreation result in the example system is appeared in Table 1.

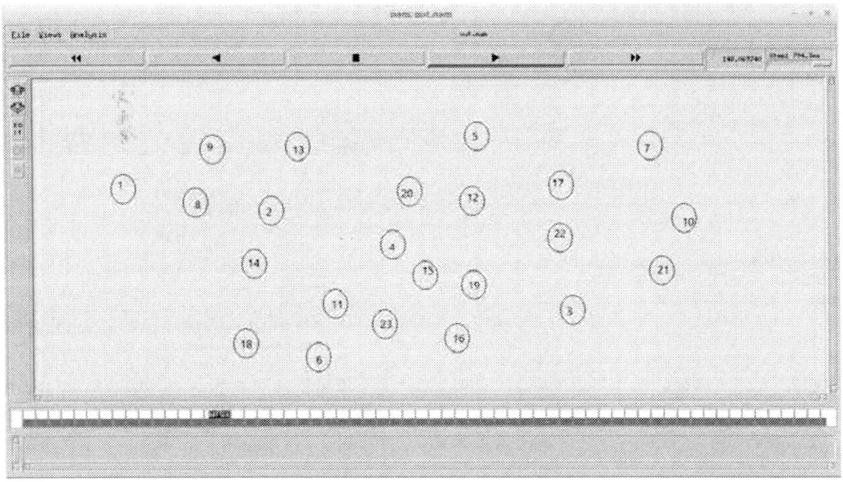

Figure 3. A sample network

Table1. The node's number selected as destination node in sample network, the transmission range of a node is 100m

The number of destinations	Formulation	Multi-destination aware Minimum Depth Tree
1	5	5
2	7,12	6,9
3	4,11,17	0,13,14
4	4,10,11,17	4,10,11,17

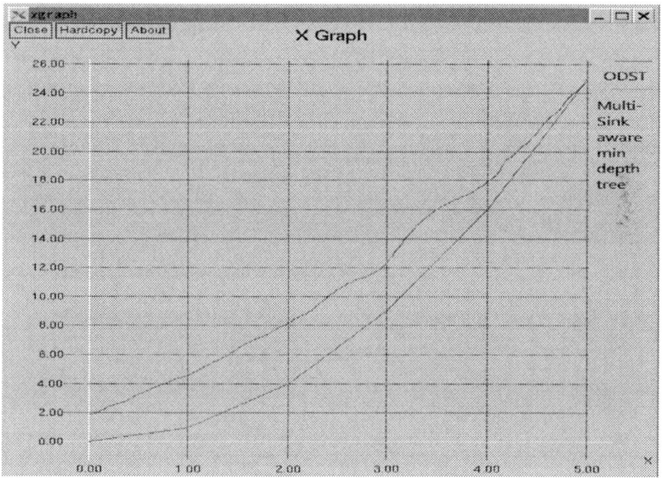

Figure 4. The comparison of in fully-connected network

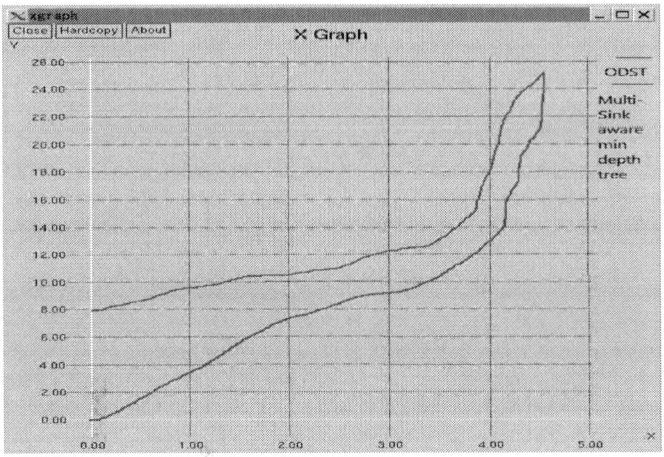

Figure 5. The comparison of when the transmission range of sensor node is 100 meters

In spite of the fact that the hub's number to be chosen as destination hub is the same as when there is just a single destination hub, the outcome demonstrates that there is a distinction in chose sensor hubs as destination hubs between Formulation with ODST and multi-destination aware Minimum Depth Tree in the event that that the quantity of destination hubs is 2, 3, 4 or 5. Figure 4 demonstrates the examination of V_{Min} in completely associated organizes. Figure 5 demonstrates the correlation of V_{Min} when the transmission scope of sensor hub is 100 meters. This is on the grounds that multi-destination aware Minimum Depth Tree permits a sensor hub to choose just a single way which is the most limited way to speak with the destination hub. In the multi-destination, aware Minimum Depth Tree calculation, sensor hubs around destination hub dependably expend more vitality than hubs a long way from the destination hub. In this way, sensor hubs a long way from the destination hub can't send information to the destination hub regardless of the possibility that they have a ton of vitality.

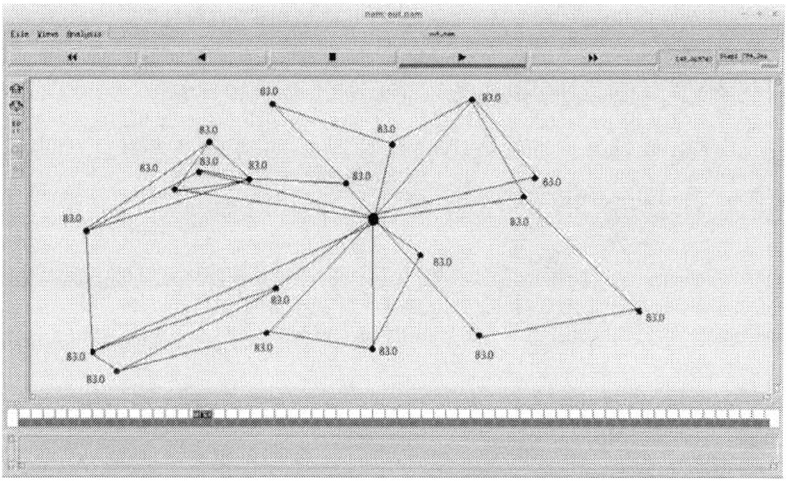

Figure 6. Routing paths and data volume by Formulation with ODST in fully-connected network, the number is data volume produced by each sensor node

The proposed definition with ODST in the manuscript essentially builds V_{Min} by utilizing numerous ways for correspondences and by conceding decided information volume to each connection. On the off chance that there is just a single destination hub in a completely associated organize, the V_{Min} by proposed detailing, is around 3 times greater than the V_{Min} by multi-destination aware Minimum Depth Tree. The reason that the area of the destination hub chose by every calculation is diverse is likewise brought on by whether multi-way is accessible or not. This implies the maximum/min conspire functions admirably for reasonableness in the situation, and system decency is expanded to contrast and multi-destination aware Minimum Depth Tree. Since multi-destination aware Minimum Depth Tree arranges the system into tree engineering, there is a wide distinction of the information volume created by every hub.

The proposed method overcomes the latency issue which affects most of the Internet based WSN. Even though the communication channel varies the algorithm is robust enough to handle the same without any blocking. The data loss due to excessive fragmentation and reassembly is reduced drastically. The algorithm is also capable of handling the frequent change in the routing topology

CHAPTER 7

CONCLUSION

The idea of occasion to-destination dependability is essential for re-at-risk transport of occasion elements in Wireless Sensor Networks. This is because of the way that the destination is just intrigued by the aggregate data of various source hubs and not in individual sensor reports. This is likewise the motivation behind why conventional end-to-end dependability thoughts and transport arrangements are improper for Wireless Sensor Networks. In light of such an aggregate unwavering quality idea, another solid transport plot for Wireless Sensor Networks, the Occurrence to Destination Stable Transport Protocol (ODST) convention, is exhibited in the manuscript. Occurrence to Destination Stable Transport Protocol (ODST) is a novel transport arrangement created to accomplish dependable occasion recognition with least vitality use and blockage determination usefulness. Occurrence to Destination Stable Transport Protocol (ODST) has been customized to meet the one-of-a-kind prerequisite of Wireless Sensor Networks. Its clog control part fills the double need of accomplishing dependability and rationing vitality. The calculations of Occurrence to Destination Stable Transport Protocol (ODST) basically keep running on the destination and require negligible usefulness at asset obliged sensor hubs. The essential target of Occurrence to Destination Stable Transport Protocol (ODST) is to arrange the net-function as close as conceivable to the ideal working point, where the required unwavering quality is accomplished with least vitality utilization and without system blockage. In this way, Occurrence to Destination Stable Transport Protocol (ODST) convention operation is controlled by the present system state in view of the dependability accomplished and the congestion condition.

REFERENCES

[1] Atzori, Luigi, Antonio Iera, and Giacomo Morabito. "The internet of things: A survey." Computer networks 54, no. 15 (2010): 2787-2805.

[2] Bellavista, Paolo, Giuseppe Cardone, Antonio Corra

[3]

[4] di, and Luca Foschini. "Convergence of MANET and WSN in IoT urban scenarios." IEEE Sensors Journal 13, no. 10 (2013): 3558-3567.

[5] Cardone, Giuseppe, Antonio Corradi, and Luca Foschini. "Cross-network opportunistic collection of urgent data in wireless sensor networks." The Computer Journal (2011): bxr043.

[6] Dutta, Prabal, David E. Culler, and Scott Shenker. "Procrastination Might Lead to a Longer and More Useful Life." In HotNets. 2007.

[7] Filipponi, Luca, Andrea Vitaletti, Giada Landi, Vincenzo Memeo, Giorgio Laura, and Paolo Pucci. "Smart city: An event driven architecture for monitoring public spaces with heterogeneous sensors." In Sensor Technologies and Applications (SENSORCOMM), 2010 Fourth International Conference on, pp. 281-286. IEEE, 2010.

[8] Foschini, Luca, Tarik Taleb, Antonio Corradi, and Dario Bottazzi. "M2M-based metropolitan platform for IMS-enabled road traffic management in IoT." IEEE Communications Magazine 49, no. 11 (2011).

[9] Gnawali, Omprakash, Rodrigo Fonseca, Kyle Jamieson, David Moss, and Philip Levis. "Collection tree protocol." In Proceedings of the 7th ACM conference on embedded networked sensor systems, pp. 1-14. ACM, 2009.

[10] Herberg, Ulrich, and Thomas Clausen. "Study of multipoint-to-point and broadcast traffic performance in the "IPv6 Routing Protocol for Low Power and Lossy Networks"." Journal of Ambient Intelligence and Humanized Computing 2, no. 4 (2011): 293-305.

[11] Lee, Jaeseung, Yunsick Sung, and Jong Hyuk Park. "Lightweight Sensor Authentication Scheme for Energy Efficiency in Ubiquitous Computing Environments." Sensors 16, no. 12 (2016): 2044.

[12] Liu, Chi Harold, Jun Fan, Joel W. Branch, and Kin K. Leung. "Toward qoi and energy-efficiency in internet-of-things sensory environments." IEEE Transactions on Emerging Topics in Computing 2, no. 4 (2014): 473-487.

[13] Muruganathan, Siva D., Daniel CF Ma, Rolly I. Bhasin, and Abraham O. Fapojuwo. "A centralized energy-efficient routing protocol for wireless sensor networks." IEEE Communications Magazine 43, no. 3 (2005): S8-13.

[14] Yovanof, Gregory S., and George N. Hazapis. "An architectural framework and enabling wireless technologies for digital cities & intelligent urban environments." Wireless personal communications 49, no. 3 (2009): 445-463.

[15] Zhong, Lizhi C., Jan M. Rabaey, and Adam Wolisz. "Does proper coding make single hop wireless sensor networks reality: the power consumption perspective." In Wireless Communications and Networking Conference, 2005 IEEE, vol. 2, pp. 664-669. IEEE, 2005.

[16] Zorzi, Michele, Alexander Gluhak, Sebastian Lange, and Alessandro Bassi. "From today's intranet of things to a future internet of things: a wireless-and mobility-related view." IEEE Wireless Communications 17, no. 6 (2010).

Publisher: Eliva Press Global Ltd

Email: info@elivapress.com

Made in United States
Orlando, FL
04 November 2026

90209885R00024